BENJAMIN LEES

DIALOGUE

for cello and piano

BOOSEY&HAWKES

DISTRIBUTED BY

HAL•LEONARD®
CORPORATION

7777 W. BLUEMOUND RD. P.O. BOX 13819 MILWAUKEE, WI 53213

www.boosey.com
www.halleonard.com

Commissioned by The Clark-Schuldmann Duo

First performed 2 March, 1977
at the 92nd Street Y, New York City
by The Clark-Schuldmann Duo
Harry Clark, cello
Sanda Schuldmann, piano

Duration: *ca.* 10 min.

to Harry Clark and Sanda Schuldman

DIALOGUE
for Cello and Piano

BENJAMIN LEES
1977

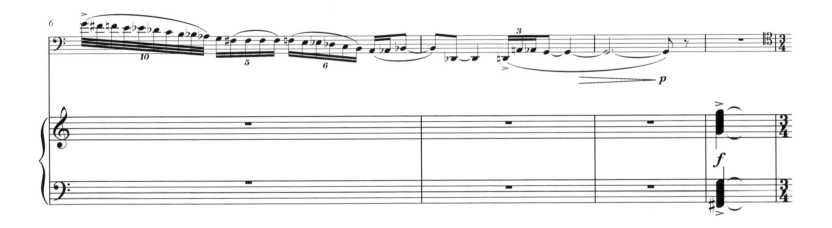

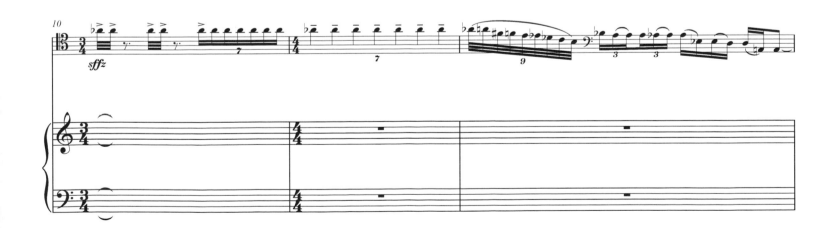

* Palm clusters

M 051-10609-7

4

DIALOGUE
for Cello and Piano

Cello

BENJAMIN LEES
1977

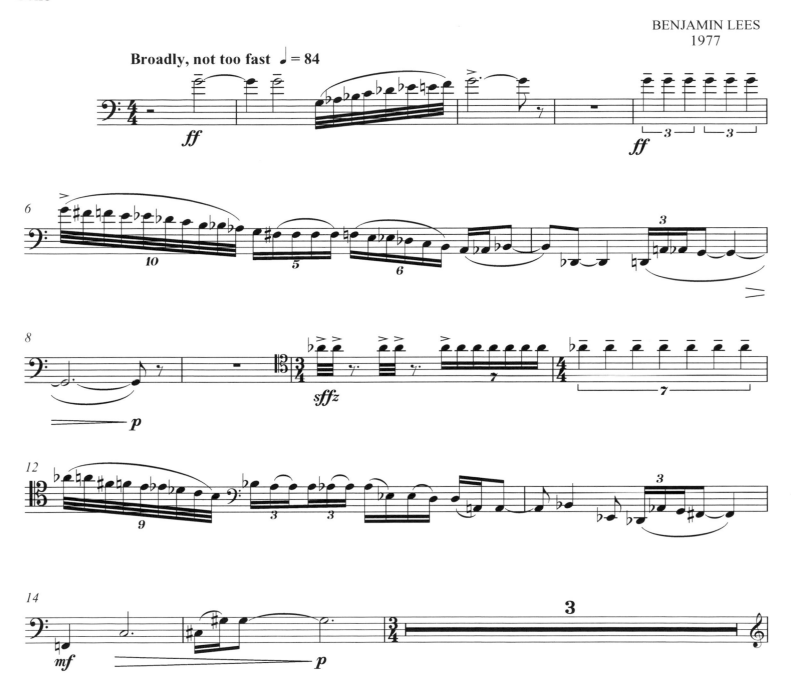

M 051-10609-7

2

Cello

February 6, 1977
Great Neck, New York

M 051-10609-7